POM✷POM PUPPIES

Make Your Own Adorable Dogs

KLUTZ APRIL CHORBA

BUILD A NEW BEST FRIEND

How do you turn a boring ball of yarn into a puppy with personality?

Just wrap, snip, and glue — and then trim-trim-trim until your puppy takes shape.

CONTENTS

You can follow the step-by-step directions to make the specific breeds in this book, but don't feel limited by them. Once you get the hang of making pom-pom pups, it's easy to adjust the color or ears or tail or trim to make any breed of dog you want.

**4 COLORS
OF YARN**

BLACK

What

YOU GET

WHITE

BROWN

TAN

1 POM-POM MAKER
(4 PIECES)

BEAD EYES

**FOAM
NOSES & TONGUES**

GLUE

TINY BOWS

MINI POM-POMS

STYLING COMB

FELT

PUNCH-OUT CIRCLES AND EAR PATTERNS

SMALL EAR

MEDIUM EAR

LARGE EAR

PUNCH-OUT CARRIERS, COLLARS, AND OTHER ACCESSORIES

WHAT YOU NEED

SCISSORS

Scissors with thin blades like this work best.

Scissors like this are too big.

GETTING STARTED

MEASURING YARN

You can use the ruler on the back of this book to measure yarn. When measuring, keep the yarn snug, but don't pull it so tight it stretches.

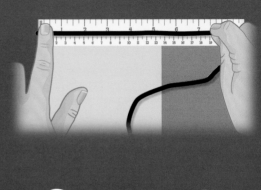

DOGGIE DIAGRAMS

To make the proper pom-poms for each puppy, just follow the charts. It takes 8 yards of yarn to make any pom-pom, but the colors will vary. The charts show exactly how much of each color to use and where.

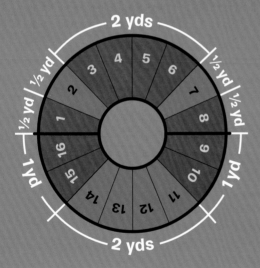

EACH NUMBERED SECTION EQUALS ½ YARD.

Of course, dogs come in all kinds of colors and patterns. If you want to swap out some of the chart colors for colors of your own choosing, go right ahead.

 SHORTCUT:

If you wrap once all the way around the height of the book, that's a ½ yard of yarn.

1 YARD
EQUALS

1 FOOT	+	1 FOOT	+	1 FOOT

EQUALS
ABOUT 1 METER

TIPS

- Dog grooming can be messy. For easy cleanup, trim your puppy over a container or a cookie sheet with raised edges to catch all the little yarn clippings.

- Dump the clippings in a storage baggie for later use. They come in handy when making spots and fluffy puffs.

- These puppies make great gifts for anyone over six years old. Do not give finished pom-pom puppies to small children.

- This book comes with enough supplies to make a litter of four puppies. When you're ready to make more, get additional supplies at klutz.com or your local craft store. Look for yarn labeled "super bulky."

READY?

Start by making a short-haired dog (on page 14). It's the best way to learn the pom-pom puppy basics.

MAKING POM·POMS

It takes two pom-poms to make a pup—one for the head and one for the body. The wrapping patterns, yarn length, and colors will vary, but the basic pom-pom is always the same.

TO GET THE HANG OF POM-POM MAKING, START WITH A SIMPLE TAN ONE.

YOU'LL NEED:

3 PIECES OF TAN YARN
- 2 pieces, 4 yards (4 m) each
- 1 piece, ½ yard (0.5 m)

THE POM-POM MAKER SCISSORS

1 The pom-pom maker comes in four sections — two sections with bumps and two with holes. Line up one of the bumpy sections with one of the holey sections, with the bent feet facing out.

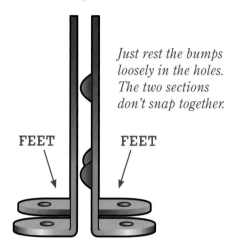

Just rest the bumps loosely in the holes. The two sections don't snap together.

FEET

FEET

2 Now you'll hold the sections together by wrapping them with yarn. Press the end of a 4-yard (4 m) piece of yarn against the center of the arch.

Let about ½ inch (1.25 cm) of yarn hang over the top of the arch.

3 Wrap the yarn around both sections once, crossing over the tail...

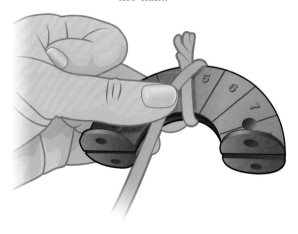

...then wrap around again, crossing over the tail in an X pattern to secure it.

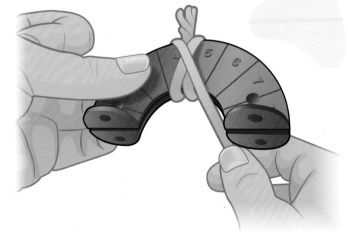

4 Now, wrap the yarn around the arch in fairly even rows. Once you reach the end, start wrapping in the other direction, overlapping the wraps you just made.

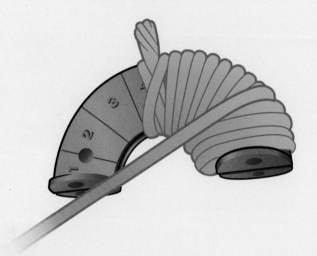

5 Continue wrapping until the entire arch is covered fairly evenly and all the yarn is wrapped.

Wrap right over the tail to flatten it.

6 Tuck the loose end securely under some of the wrapped yarn.

If you can't lift the yarn with your fingers, try using the handle of your comb.

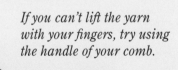

7 Repeat steps 1–6 with the other 4-yard length of yarn on the other half of the pom-pom maker.

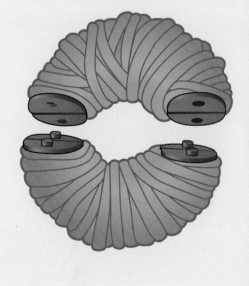

8 Snap the feet of the wrapped arches together.

Make sure all four feet are securely attached.

9 Find the groove between one set of feet and insert a blade of your scissors as far as it will go.

Don't push the blade down toward the center of the pom-pom maker. Run it along the groove around the edge instead.

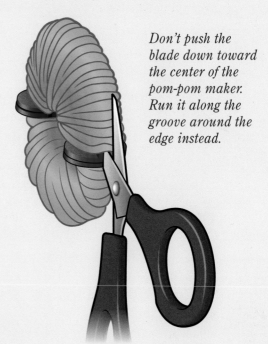

10 Cut along the groove around the entire circle.

As you cut, the yarn pieces will fill in the center of the pom-pom maker.

DON'T WORRY — THEY WON'T FALL OUT!

11 Rest the pom-pom maker on a flat surface. Wedge the ½-yard (0.5-m) piece of yarn into the groove and pull it snug.

It can be tricky to get the yarn into the groove, but you can do it.

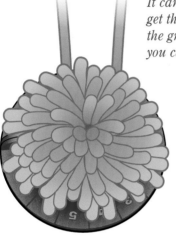

12 Tie the strand in a knot, pulling the ends firmly so the knot slides down into the groove and holds the center of the pom-pom together.

Tie it tight!

13 Pull the ends of the strand to the opposite side and tie another tight knot there.

It's important to pull the knots tight so your pom-poms will stay together when it's time to transform them into puppies.

14 Tie one more knot in the same spot, just to be sure.

15 Remove the pom-pom maker by popping the pieces apart.

16 Trim the long strands of yarn so they match the rest of the pom-pom. Set them aside for now — you will use these scrap pieces later when making puppies.

DOGGONE IT! YOU DID IT!

MULTICOLORED POM-POMS

WHEN THE CHART CALLS FOR MORE THAN ONE COLOR OF YARN, KEEP THESE TIPS IN MIND:

- Every color change on the chart is made by wrapping a separate piece of yarn. Start each piece of yarn in the center of each colored section, and wrap as usual.

- When you tie the center of the pom-pom together, make sure the tails of the knotted yarn come out among strands of the same color.

CHIHUAHUA

Make a nearly life-sized version of this teacup pup.

YOU'LL NEED:

- 1 head pom-pom (see chart)
- 1 body pom-pom (see chart)
- 1 scrap of yarn, any color but tan, about 1 foot (0.3 m)
- 2 bead eyes
- 1 foam nose
- 1 tan mini pom-pom
- tan felt
- the Medium Ear pattern piece
- 1 tan punch-out circle

HEAD POM-POM

3 PIECES OF YARN

- 2 tan, 4 yards (4 m) each
- 1 tan to tie the middle, ½ yard (0.5 m)

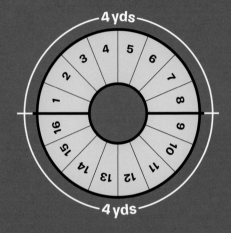

BODY POM-POM

3 PIECES OF YARN

- 2 tan, 4 yards (4 m) each
- 1 tan to tie the middle, ½ yard (0.5 m)

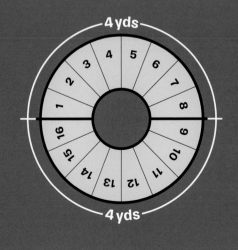

See pages 8–13 for pom-pom making instructions.

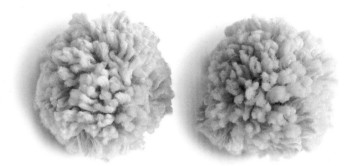

MAKE A HEAD

1 On one of the pom-poms, pinch a tuft of about 20 strands of yarn.

Don't worry about getting precisely 20 pieces — the count doesn't have to be exact.

2 Tie the scrap of yarn around the tuft.

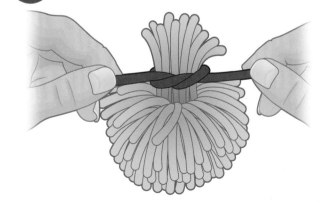

3 Grab the tuft like a handle and trim the rest of the yarn short. Keep trimming until all the strands look about the same length, forming a nice, round ball.

Don't be shy about cutting the yarn short — remember, this will be a short-haired dog. As long as you trim the ball evenly all the way around, it'll look great.

Don't cut this!

4 Untie the tuft and part it into two equal sections.

5 Looking directly down at the tuft, glob a little glue near the top of the part.

6 Stick the mini pom-pom in the glue. Wait a minute for it to set before moving on.

THIS IS THE PUPPY'S MUZZLE.

7 Rotate the pom-pom so the muzzle faces you. Now you'll make the cheeks. Imagine that the mini pom-pom is the tip of a triangle. Trim the tufts along the imaginary triangle's sides.

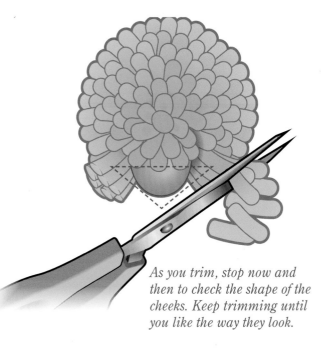

As you trim, stop now and then to check the shape of the cheeks. Keep trimming until you like the way they look.

8 Glue the foam nose near the top of the mini pom-pom. Let the glue dry for a minute before moving on.

9 Use your fingertip to make two dents in the pom-pom where you want the eyes to go. Put a dot of glue in each dent, and then stick the beads in place.

Make sure the holes are on the sides of the beads.

10 Cut a piece of felt that's a little larger than the Medium Ear pattern.

11 Holding the pattern against the felt piece, carefully trim around the ear shape.

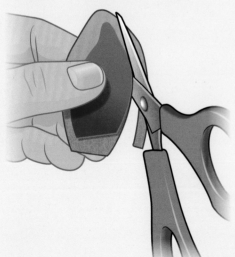

12 Repeat to make a second ear.

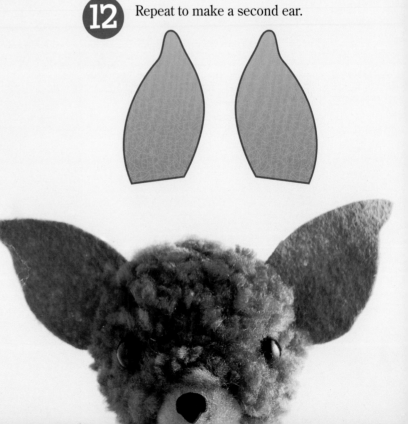

ATTACHING EARS

BECAUSE PUPS ARE SO FUZZY, IT CAN BE TRICKY TO GLUE EARS SO THEY STAY PUT.

It's easiest if you use your fingertip to make a dent in the pom-pom where you want the ear to go, and then put a drop of glue in the dent.

Stick the ear in the glue. Pinch the base of the ear so the felt is folded in half lengthwise. Press the surrounding yarn against the folded ear and hold it until the glue is set.

13   Glue the ears in place.

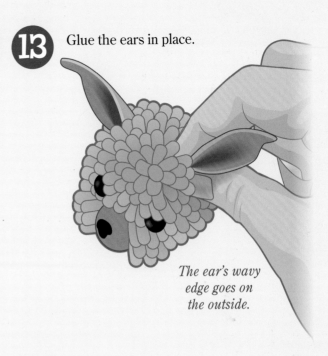

The ear's wavy edge goes on the outside.

14   Take a look at your puppy's head and trim any fur that seems out of place.

PUT THE HEAD ASIDE. TIME TO MOVE ON TO THE BODY.

MAKE A BODY

15 Tie the scrap yarn around the middle of the body pom-pom. Trim all the yarn on one side of the scrap so it matches the head pom-pom. Untie the scrap when you're done trimming.

Leave the yarn on the other half of the pom-pom long.

16 Separate the untrimmed half into three equal sections as shown.

17 Holding the two side sections flat, trim just the center section so it matches the short half. You'll end up with two tufts of long yarn, separated by trimmed yarn.

THIS IS THE PUPPY'S BELLY.

18 Rotate the pom-pom so the long tufts are on the top and bottom. Divide the bottom tuft into three equal sections, and trim the center one.

NOW THE BELLY IS HERE.

THESE ARE TWO OF THE PUPPY'S PAWS.

19 Repeat step 18 with the top tuft to make the puppy's other two paws.

20 Set the body on its paws. Trim any fur that looks out of place.

IF YOU ACCIDENTALLY CUT THE PAWS TOO SMALL, JUST COMB THEM OUT TO MAKE THEM FLUFFY. NO ONE WILL KNOW THE DIFFERENCE.

PUT IT ALL TOGETHER

21 Trim the bottom of the head and the top of the body so they are flat.

22 Put a glob of glue on the punch-out circle. Use the tip of the bottle to spread the glue to the edge of the circle.

23 Stick the circle in the center of the flat section on top of the body.

24 Add more glue to the top of the circle, spreading it out to the edge as before.

25 Place the head on top of the glued circle.

Center the face above two of the paws.

26 Squish the head and body together for a minute until the glue is set.

Don't worry about hurting your pup. He'll pop right back up when you're done.

27 Let your puppy rest for several minutes, until the glue is completely dry.

He could be finished now, or you can add more detail with a felt tail or foam tongue.

IT'S UP TO YOU — HE'S YOUR PUPPY!

DOG TRICKS

SIT

If your puppy tips over instead of sitting up, try adjusting the paws. Spreading the feet farther apart will give her a more secure base.

LIE DOWN

To make a puppy that looks ready for a nap, glue the head to the front of the body, rather than the top.

BEG

Set the body on its tail, with the paws facing forward, before gluing the head on top. You'll end up with a cute little begger.

ACCESSORIZE

Glue on punch-out collars and other extras to personalize your pup.

Write your dog's name or initials on the dog tag.

STAY

If he keeps tipping over, make sure your pup's underside is nice and flat. You may need to trim it a bit.

SPEAK!

JUST KIDDING.

But you can make a pup *listen* by gluing the head at a slightly crooked angle. Finally, someone who understands everything you say.

POMERANIAN

The secret to fluff is in the combing.

YOU'LL NEED:

- 1 head pom-pom (see chart)
- 1 body pom-pom (see chart)
- 1 scrap of yarn, any color but white, about 1 foot (0.3 m)
- 2 bead eyes
- 1 foam nose
- 1 white mini pom-pom
- white felt
- the Small Ear pattern piece
- 1 white punch-out circle

HEAD POM-POM

3 PIECES OF YARN

- 2 white, 4 yards (4 m) each
- 1 white to tie the middle, ½ yard (0.5 m)

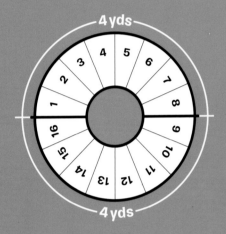

BODY POM-POM

3 PIECES OF YARN

- 2 white, 4 yards (4 m) each
- 1 white to tie the middle, ½ yard (0.5 m)

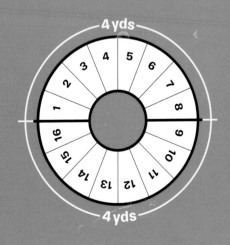

See pages 8–13 for pom-pom making instructions.

1 Tie a tuft on one of the white pom-poms and trim the rest of the yarn short to form a nice, round ball (pages 15–16, steps 1–3).

2 With the tuft still tied, pinch a small section of the untied yarn as close to the center of the ball as you can. (Pinching the yarn keeps it from being pulled out by the comb.) Comb out the section to make it fluffy.

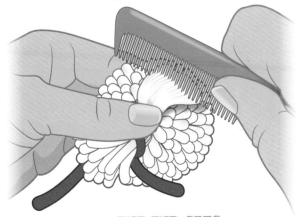

THE FUR GETS
FLUFFIER THE MORE
YOU COMB IT.

3 Fluff out the rest of the ball the same way, pinching and combing section by section.

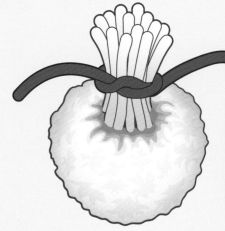

IT'S OKAY IF A COUPLE STRANDS OF YARN COME OUT DURING COMBING. THE FLUFFINESS WILL MAKE UP FOR IT.

4 Now untie the tuft and part it into two equal sections.

5 Fluff each half, combing away from the center part.

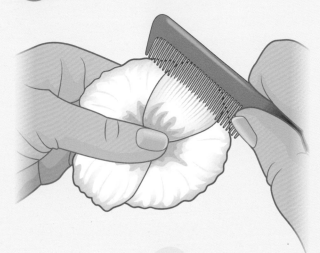

6 Glue the white mini pom-pom in place to make the muzzle (pages 16–17, steps 5–6).

7 Trim the cheeks as you like. You can clip them at an angle...

...or leave them super fluffy.

8 Attach the nose and eyes (pages 17–18, steps 8–9).

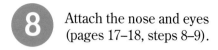

9 Cut ears out of the white felt, using the Small Ear pattern piece, and then glue them in place (pages 18–19).

10 Use the other white pom-pom to make a body as shown on pages 20–21.

11 Carefully comb out the entire body — paws and all.

Remember to pinch the base of the yarn as you comb.

12 Glue the head to the body using the white punch-out circle (pages 22–23).

13 After the glue is completely dry, give your puppy a final fluff (and trim, if needed).

HERE COMES TROUBLE...

Princess Cupcake

PUG

Wrapping the pom-pom maker with different yarn colors makes it easy to create a cute-as-a-bug pug.

YOU'LL NEED:

- 1 head pom-pom (see chart)
- 1 body pom-pom (see chart)
- 2 scraps of yarn, any color but tan, about 1 foot (0.3 m) each
- 2 bead eyes
- 1 foam nose
- black felt
- the Medium Ear pattern piece
- 1 tan punch-out circle
- tan felt

HEAD POM-POM

5 PIECES OF YARN

- 1 tan, 4 yards (4 m)
- 1 tan, 1½ yards (1.5 m)
- 1 black, ½ yard (0.5 m)
- 1 tan, 2 yards (2 m)
- 1 tan to tie the middle, ½ yard (0.5 m)

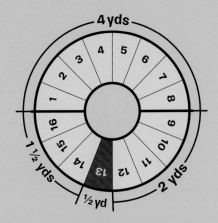

BODY POM-POM

3 PIECES OF YARN

- 2 tan, 4 yards (4 m) each
- 1 tan to tie the middle, ½ yard (0.5 m)

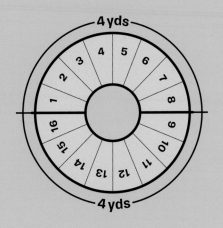

1 Trim the entire head pom-pom to a short, even length. Then bunch all the black yarn together in a U-shape as shown.

2 Glue on the eyes and nose, and use the Medium Ear pattern piece to cut ears in the black felt (page 18). This time, keep the ears flat, not folded, as you glue them in place (page 19).

NOW MAKE THE EARS FLOPPY.

Turn the page to find out how.

See pages 8–13 for pom-pom making instructions.

FLOPPY EARS

To make any pup's ears flop, start by putting a dot of glue on the front of each ear tip.

Bend the ears forward and tie a scrap of yarn around the entire head, like a sweatband, to glue them down. Don't remove the scrap until the dog is completely finished.

3 Make the body, and then glue the body and head together (pages 20–23).

4 Cut a circle out of the tan felt, and then trim it into a spiral shape. Glue it into place as the pug's tail.

You can cut around one of the punch-out circles to make the circle.

5 Untie the scrap yarn sweatband and reshape the head with your fingers.

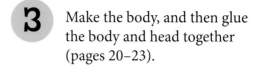

NOW HUG THAT PUG!

DIFFERENT COLORS = DIFFERENT BREEDS
MEET THE BOSTON TERRIER

BEAGLE

To be a beagle, all you need
are cute floppy ears and
an excitable attitude.

YOU'LL NEED:

- 1 head pom-pom (see chart)
- 1 body pom-pom (see chart)
- 2 scraps of tan yarn about
  1 foot (0.3 m) each
- 2 bead eyes
- 1 white mini pom-pom
- 1 foam nose
- black felt
- the Large Ear pattern piece
- 1 black punch-out circle

HEAD POM-POM

7 PIECES OF YARN

- 2 brown, ½ yard (0.5 m) each
- 1 black, 3 yards (3 m)
- 2 brown, 1½ yards (1.5 m) each
- 1 white, 1 yard (1 m)
- 1 brown to tie the middle, ½ yard (0.5 m)

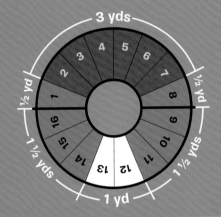

BODY POM-POM

5 PIECES OF YARN

- 2 brown, 1 yard (1 m) each
- 1 black, 2 yards (2 m)
- 1 white, 4 yards (4 m)
- 1 white to tie the middle, ½ yard (0.5 m)

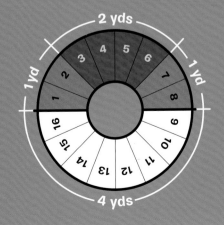

 On the head pom-pom, separate about eight pieces of white yarn. Use a scrap of yarn to tie the rest of the white together in a tuft.

2 Grab the tuft like a handle and trim the rest of the yarn short, so it forms a nice, round ball.

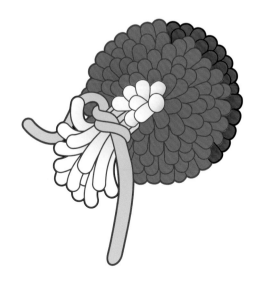

See pages 8–13 for pom-pom making instructions.

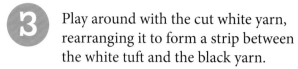

3 Play around with the cut white yarn, rearranging it to form a strip between the white tuft and the black yarn.

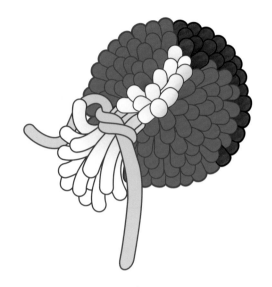

4 Untie the tuft, part it down the middle, and glue the mini pom-pom in place to make the muzzle (pages 16–17, steps 4–7). Trim the cheeks as you like.

5 Glue on the eyes and nose, and use the Large Ear pattern piece to cut ears in the black felt (page 18). Keep the ears flat, not folded, as you glue them in place (page 19).

6 Glue and tie the ear tips down to make them floppy (page 34). Leave the head to dry.

7 Make the body with the other pom-pom. Start by tying the other scrap of yarn around the middle, roughly separating the white side from the black-and-brown side. Follow the steps on pages 20–21, trimming the black-and-brown half first, so the puppy's back will be mostly dark and the paws will be mostly white.

8 Attach the head (pages 22–23). When the glue is dry, untie the scrap yarn sweatband and reshape the head with your fingers.

GO FETCH!

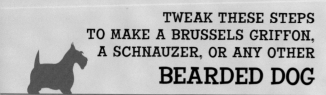
SCOTTIE

Whether your Scottie is a boy or a girl, the beard is always a good look.

YOU'LL NEED:

- 1 head pom-pom (see chart)
- 1 body pom-pom (see chart)
- 1 scrap of yarn, any color but black, about 1 foot (0.3 m)
- 2 bead eyes
- 1 foam nose
- black felt
- the Small Ear pattern piece
- 1 black punch-out circle

HEAD POM-POM

3 PIECES OF YARN

- 2 black, 4 yards (4 m) each
- 1 black to tie the middle, ½ yard (0.5 m)

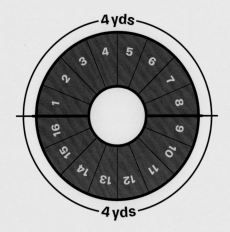

BODY POM-POM

3 PIECES OF YARN

- 2 black, 4 yards (4 m) long
- 1 black to tie the middle, ½ yard (0.5 m)

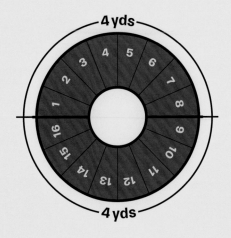

1 Tie the scrap of yarn around the middle of one of the pom-poms. Trim short all the yarn on one side of the scrap. Untie the scrap when you're done trimming.

Leave the yarn on the other half of the pom-pom long.

2 Divide the long section into two equal parts.

See pages 8–13 for pom-pom making instructions.

3 Trim one of the long sections to match the short yarn.

4 Divide the remaining section into two equal parts.

5 Trim another one of the long sections short. The remaining long section will be the puppy's beard.

6 Comb out the beard to make it fuzzy.

Pinch the base of the yarn as you comb so you don't pull any pieces out.

7 Neaten up the beard by trimming any strands that look out of place.

8 Glue on the nose just above the middle of the beard. Then finish the head with eyes and small ears cut from the black felt (pages 18–19).

9 Make the body, and then glue the body and the head together (pages 20–23).

Use tiny scraps for fuzzy eyebrows (see page 53).

Comb out the paws so they are extra fluffy.

DIFFERENT COLORS = DIFFERENT BREEDS
MEET THE BRUSSELS GRIFFON

BORDER COLLIE

Warning:
This masked bandit
will steal your heart.

YOU'LL NEED:

- 1 head pom-pom (see chart)
- 1 body pom-pom (see chart)
- 1 scrap of yarn, any color but black or white, about 1 foot (0.3 m)
- 2 bead eyes
- 1 foam nose
- 1 white mini pom-pom
- black felt
- the Medium Ear pattern piece
- 1 black punch-out circle

HEAD POM-POM

7 PIECES OF YARN

- 4 black, 1½ yards (1.5 m) each
- 2 white, 1 yard (1 m) each
- 1 black to tie the middle, ½ yard (0.5 m)

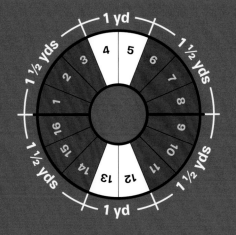

BODY POM-POM

3 PIECES OF YARN

- 1 black, 4 yards (4 m) long
- 1 white, 4 yards (4 m) long
- 1 white to tie the middle, ½ yard (0.5 m)

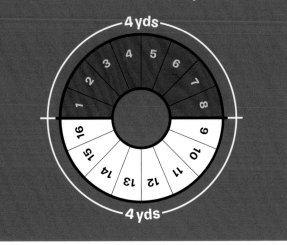

① Tie the scrap of yarn around the middle of the head pom-pom so there is one white section on each side. Trim all the yarn short on one side of the scrap. Untie the scrap when you're done trimming.

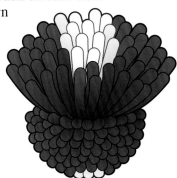

② On the untrimmed side, separate about seven pieces of white yarn. Use the scrap of yarn to tie the rest of the white together in a tuft.

③ With the tuft facing up, divide the rest of the untrimmed yarn into four roughly equal sections — one on the top, one on the bottom, and one on each side.

IT SHOULD LOOK LIKE A PLUS SIGN.

See pages 8–13 for pom-pom making instructions.

4 Find the section of the plus sign with the most white yarn in it and trim it short. Then find the section opposite the whitest one and trim it, too.

5 Lay the head so the tied tuft points to one side and one section of untrimmed yarn is facing up. Split that yarn vertically down the center, and trim short the half that is closest to the tuft.

Repeat on the other side, flipping the head so the tuft points in the opposite direction.

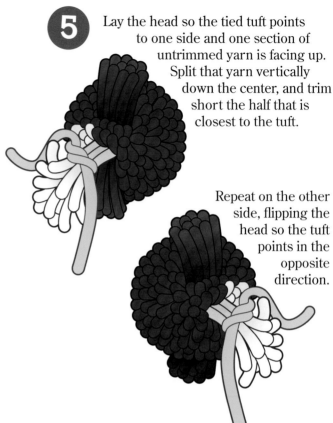

6 Carefully comb out the untrimmed yarn on both sides of the tuft.

Pinch the base of the yarn as you comb so you don't pull any pieces out.

7 Play around with the cut white yarn until it forms a streak stretching to the tuft.

8 Untie the tuft. Complete the head, adding a mini pom-pom muzzle, nose, eyes, and medium-sized black felt ears (pages 16–19, steps 4–14).

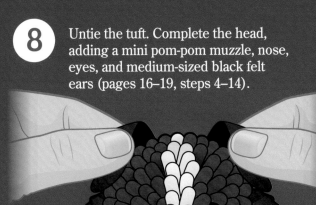

After the ears are dry, fold them forward — pressing them for a few seconds so the bend will stay.

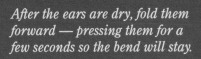

9 Make the body with the other pom-pom. Start by tying the scrap of yarn around the middle, roughly separating the black and white sides. Follow the steps on pages 20–21, trimming the black half first, so the puppy's back will be mostly black and the paws will be mostly white.

10 When the body is finished, comb out the paws to make them fluffy. Play around with the yarn so there is some white fur on the puppy's chest, between the front paws.

11 Glue the head to the body using the black circle (pages 22–23).

DID YOU TAKE THE DOG OUT?

YORKIE

Go ahead, share your secrets.
This puppy is all ears.

YOU'LL NEED:

- 1 head pom-pom (see chart)
- 1 body pom-pom (see chart)
- 1 scrap of yarn, any color but black or brown, about 1 foot (0.3 m)
- 2 bead eyes
- 1 foam nose
- 1 black punch-out circle

HEAD POM-POM

9 PIECES OF YARN

- 2 black, ½ yard (0.5 m) each
- 2 brown, ½ yard (0.5 m) each
- 1 black, 2 yards (2 m)
- 2 black, 1 yard (1 m) each
- 1 brown, 2 yards (2 m)
- 1 black to tie the middle, ½ yard (0.5 m)

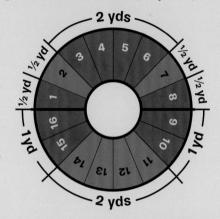

BODY POM-POM

3 PIECES OF YARN

- 1 black, 4 yards (4 m)
- 1 brown, 4 yards (4 m)
- 1 black to tie the middle, ½ yard (0.5 m)

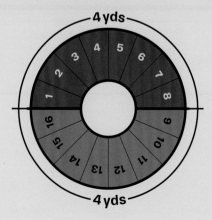

See pages 8–13 for pom-pom making instructions.

1 On the head pom-pom, trim all the black yarn short. Leave the brown yarn long.

THESE WILL BE THE EARS.

THIS WILL BE THE BEARD.

2 Hold the pom-pom so the beard is on top, and one of the ears is pointing at you.

3 Split the beard vertically down the center. Trim the right half short.

4 Split the remaining long section of the beard vertically down the center. Trim the left half short.

5 Carefully comb out the entire pom-pom — black and brown, long and short — a small section at a time…

…so it looks like this.

Pinch the base of the yarn you comb so you don't pull out any pieces.

6 Holding the pom-pom upright, with the ears on top, play around with the yarn to form a black streak down into the center of the trimmed brown area just above the beard.

7 Glue the nose to the base of the black streak, and then glue on the eyes (page 18, step 9). After the head is completely dry, comb and clip the ears and beard to shape them any way you like.

8 Make the body with the other pom-pom. Start by tying the scrap of yarn around the middle, roughly separating the black and brown sides. Follow the steps on pages 20–21, trimming the black half first, so the puppy's back will be mostly black and the paws will be mostly brown.

9 When the body is finished, comb it out to make it fluffy. Play around with the yarn so there is some brown fur on the puppy's chest, between the front paws.

10 Glue the head to the body using the black circle (pages 22–23).

YOU CAN ADD A SCRAP OF YARN TO MAKE A LITTLE PONYTAIL ON YOUR YORKIE'S HEAD. TURN THE PAGE TO FIND OUT HOW.

GRRR!

GRRR!

ADDING SPOTS

THESE DOGS ARE JUST BEGGING FOR YARN SCRAPS FROM THE TABLE.

Add speckles and spots by gluing tiny yarn clippings directly into the fur. The handle of the comb can help you push the clippings deep into the pom-pom.

MINIATURE PINSCHER

DALMATIAN

ADDING POOFS

PONYTAIL
Tie a knot at one end of a long scrap.

FLOWING EARS
Tie several scraps together at one end.

POODLE 'DO
Tie several scraps together in the middle.

FLUFF THE POOFS BY CAREFULLY COMBING THE YARN AWAY FROM THE KNOT. GLUE THE KNOT DIRECTLY INTO THE POM-POM.

SHIH TZU

COCKER SPANIEL

POODLE

PAPILLON

Credits

ART DIRECTOR APRIL CHORBA

EDITOR KAREN PHILLIPS

ILLUSTRATORS JIM KOPP, JERRY LOFARO

PHOTOGRAPHERS KATRINE NALEID, RORY EARNSHAW

PACKAGE DESIGNER DAVID AVIDOR

PRODUCTION EDITOR JEN MILLS

PRODUCTION COORDINATORS PATTY MORRIS, LINDA OLBOURNE

EDITORIAL ASSISTANT DAN LETCHWORTH

SPECIAL THANKS
ARMIN BAUTISTA, MARTINE CAMEAU, MADELEINE ROBINS,
DEBBI SIZEMORE, QUILLON TSANG